TRANSITIONS

TRANSITIONS

POSITIVE CHANGE IN YOUR LIFE & WORK

Dr. Barrie Hopson
and Mike Scally

Pfeiffer & COMPANY

Amsterdam • Johannesburg • London
San Diego • Sydney • Toronto

Published in association with

Publisher: Pfeiffer/Mercury Books

Published in the UK by Mercury Books.
This edition published by:
Pfeiffer & Company
8517 Production Avenue
San Diego, CA 92121-2280
USA

Editor: JoAnn Padgett
Page Compositor: Judy Whalen
Cover: John Odam Design Associates

Library of Congress Cataloging in Publication Data
Transitions: positive change in your life & work/Barrie Hopson and Mike Scally,
p. cm.
ISBN 0-89384-212-5 (pbk.)
1. Change (Psychology)—Problems, exercises, etc. 2. Life change events—Psychological aspects—Problems, exercises, etc. 3. Stress management. I. Scally, Mike. II. Title.
BF637.C4H67 1993
158'.1—dc20 92-50991

Printed in the United States of America.
Printing 1 2 3 4 5 6 7 8 9 10

Contents

Preface

Welcome to our series of open learning workbooks! In this brief preface, we invite you to consider some of our beliefs.

We do not need teachers to learn! Not all of what we know in life is learned through formal education. We can, and do, learn in a wide range of ways, and we learn best when we know our own needs.

The best way to help people is to encourage them to help themselves. Self-help and self-management avoid the dependency that blocks development and burdens ourselves and others.

Awareness, knowledge, and skills give us more options in life. Lack of any of these is a disadvantage; possession of them allows us to live fuller lives, shaping events rather than simply reacting.

The more able and accomplished we become, the more we fill society's reservoir of talent and contribute to the common good.

It has been said that the future is not what is used to be! In this age, the goalposts keep being moved, so increasingly our security needs to come from having information and skills.

The term "lifeskill" came from work based on these beliefs, which we began at Leeds University in the 1970s. Our philosophy has been widely applied in education, in industry and commerce, and in the community, inviting people to take charge of their lives and make them satisfying and rewarding.

Lifeskills have, so far, been available through training courses and teaching programs. Now they are available in a self-help format that is consistent with the Lifeskills approach, because you are in charge of your own learning. Learn at your own pace, in your own time, and apply your learning to your situation. We wish you enjoyment and success!

Barrie Hopson
Mike Scally

Introduction

This book is for people who care about personal development. It involves reading and doing, so we have written it as an open learning workbook.

Open learning describes a study program that is designed to adapt to the needs of individual learners. Some open learning programs involve attendance at a study center of some kind, or contact with a tutor or mentor, but even then attendance times are flexible and suit the individual. This workbook is for you to use at home or at work. Most of the activities are for you to complete alone. Sometimes we may suggest that you talk with a friend or colleague—self-development is easier if there is another person with whom to talk over ideas. But this isn't essential by any means.

With this workbook you can

- Organize your study to suit your own needs.
- Study the material alone or with other people.
- Work through the book at your own pace.
- Start and finish just where and when you want to, although we have indicated some suggested stopping points with a ☕ symbol.

The sections titled "Personal Project" involve you in more than working through the text; they require you to take additional time—sometimes an evening, sometimes a week. For this reason, we do not suggest specifically how long it will take you to complete this workbook, but the written part of the book will probably take you about six hours to complete.

Objectives

After completing this book, you will be able to

- Recognize the two types of transitions
- Know the seven stages of a transition
- Understand when you are approaching and going through a major life transition
- Appreciate the stress and potential upset involved in going through a transition
- Develop your own skills and acquire additional strategies to help you and others manage transitions well
- Appreciate the positive side of transitions: They present opportunities for personal growth and development.

Use the space below to note any of these objectives that you find particularly useful. Add any of your own if they are different; what do you hope to gain from completing this book?

You might find it useful to refer back to these notes occasionally as you work through the book. Use them to keep a check on whether you really are developing the skills you want, and keep yourself on course.

Metamorphosis

Metamorphosis means a change from one thing to something else. It can involve a change of appearance, condition, character, or situation. You have metamorphosed into the person you are today. You are the product of thousands—perhaps millions—of changes, some small, some large. Some you don't even notice, and some are a shock!

Another word for change is transition—a period of change. This book will help you to cope with transitions and change by helping you understand your own thoughts and feelings about it. By working through the book at your own pace, you will be better able to understand the stages of a transition and their potential effects on you. Any change can be exciting, but it can also be confusing and worrying.

1

Transitions—Why Learn About Them?

In this chapter, we will define a transition and identify two types. You will have the opportunity to think about some of the transitions you have experienced in the past. Life includes many kinds of transitions, as the following definitions reveal.

Transition–Passage from one state, action, subject, or set of circumstances to another; a period during which one style develops into another.

–*Pocket Oxford Dictionary*

"You may suddenly feel that it is all too much hard work and that you cannot go on and would like to go home and forget about having a baby. Or you may become irritable with everyone around you and hypercritical of the help your partner is giving."

–Sheila Kitzinger writing about the transition stage of labor in *Pregnancy and Childbirth (1980).*

"In the ongoing flux of life, man undergoes many changes. Arriving, departing, growing, declining, achieving, failing—every change involves a loss and a gain. The old environment must be given up, the new accepted. People come and go, one job is lost, another begun; territory and possessions are acquired or sold; new skills are learned, old abandoned; expectations are fulfilled or hopes dashed—in all these situations the individual is faced with the need to give up one mode of life and accept another."

–A psychologist's definition—C. M. Parkes (1972)

Using the information and examples given thus far, use the following space to write down your own working definition of a transition. Feel free to use parts of the above quotes. Does anything else come to mind? A poem? An incident? If so, incorporate it into your definition.

Now that you have begun to think about what a transition is, we will look more specifically at different kinds of transitions.

The Two Types of Transition

There are two major types of transitions that we all have to cope with

1. Stages of personal development
2. Major life events

Stages of Personal Development

Roger Gould (1978) observed that in children, the passing of years is marked by their changing bodies, while in adults, it is marked by changes in mental attitude. Gould identified seven stages of adult life and what is likely to happen to the individual during each stage. As you read through them, try to remember what your life was like at each age. Can you identify when each stage began and ended? Are there any you haven't reached?

Seven Stages of Personal Development

Stages	Features
1. Pulling up roots (late teens to early 20s)	Autonomy Self-sufficiency
2. Provisional adulthood (20s)	Selection of a career Establishment of personal relationships Achievement of a place in society
3. Age 30 transition (late 20s to early 30s)	Search for personal identity Reassessment of future objectives Search for meaning in life
4. Rooting (30s)	Establishment of long-term goals Recognition in career Career success
5. Midlife transition (late 30s to early to mid-40s)	Confrontation of gap between achievement and aspirations Reexamination of career Reexamination of personal relationships
6. Reestablishment and flowering (mid-40s to 50s)	Acceptance of time as finite Confrontation of mortality Greater autonomy
7. Mellowing (50s to 60s)	Acceptance of the concept "I own myself" Fewer personal relationships Examination of present and what it means

Write anything you feel about any of the stages in the space below.

You may feel happy and satisfied with your achievements, or you may find that you feel dissatisfied with how parts of your life have gone so far. Try to remember that none of your experiences are ever wasted; they all contribute to make you uniquely *you*.

The ages we have used are approximate, but what the table shows is that transitions occur throughout our lives. As a child or teenager, you probably thought that adulthood and being "grown-up" meant being stable, being set in your ways, and knowing all the answers. But this is rarely the case. Are you the same now as you were 10 years ago? Do you expect or want to be the same 10 years from now?

Fill in the following form on this and the next page for 10 years ago and for now.

Personal Lifestyle Survey

	10 Years Ago	*Now*
Clothing Preferences		
Daytime Activities		

	10 Years Ago	*Now*
Free Time Activities		
Favorite Music/TV Program/Movie		
Closest friends and family		
Income		

Compare the two lists and note any differences below.

____

____

____

How do you feel about the differences? Note any good or bad feelings you have about the ways you have changed.

____

____

____

____

Perhaps some things have stayed the same. Are there any similarities between the two lists? Note these.

____

____

____

____

How do you feel about the similarities between now and then? Note your good or bad feelings.

____

____

____

____

Now spend a moment thinking about

- How you expect to be in 10 years
- How you would like to be in 10 years

It's good to take time to think about what you want, for then you can plan to achieve it. Use this space to record what you expect or hope to have achieved in 10 years.

____

____

____

____

____

It is quite challenging to imagine how you might be in the future. It is impossible to know how you will change or what will happen to you. This brings us to the next type of transition.

Major Life Events, Challenges, and Stress

Life is a series of challenges for us all—there's school (40,000 hours all told), perhaps your parents move or split up, friends and relatives come and go, you're an adolescent, your body changes, boyfriends, girlfriends, exams, college, work, unemployment, marriage, partner for life, divorce, apartments, houses, new job, new town, and so on.

Some people enjoy stability, while some prefer to always be on the move. But you will have the opportunity to think more about this later on in the book. Whoever you are, it is inevitable that you will be faced with major life events. And, whether you allow it to happen consciously or unconsciously, these events will almost certainly be a stimulus or a shock to your system.

These challenges in your life can be seen positively, as something to be enjoyed, experienced, and learned from, or negatively, as something daunting that you'd rather not face. They all represent periods of transition in life. Think of some challenges you have faced positively, situations in which you feel you have coped well. (A challenge can be any event in which you have had to prove yourself—it doesn't necessarily mean climbing Mount Everest!)

Challenges I have faced positively

1. ______________________________
2. ______________________________
3. ______________________________
4. ______________________________
5. ______________________________

Is there a theme that links all or most of these challenges? What is it?

____

____

Now make a list of the five most stressful things that have happened to you. Stressful events are not necessarily bad; getting married, for instance, is one of the most stressful events known to man—or to woman, mother-in-law, or father of the bride, for that matter!

Stressful times in my life

1. ____________________
2. ____________________
3. ____________________
4. ____________________
5. ____________________

Once again, is there a theme that links all or most of these events? What is it?

____

____

____

Did any of your positive challenges reappear on your stressful list? If so, why do you think that is?

____

____

____

It is likely that most of your challenges and stressful events were transitions. Reread your own definition of a transition on page 7, then review the two preceding lists and check off the events that conform to your definition of a transition.

Look at the following statistics on stress levels. The life events listed are all transitions, and it is more than likely that you will have a number of them on your two lists.

Major Life Events and Their Stress Levels (Adults Only)

Life Event	**Score out of 100**
Death of wife or husband	100
Divorce	73
Separation	65
Spending time in jail	63
Death of a close family member	63
Personal injury or illness	53
Getting married	50
Losing your job	47
A separated couple getting together again	45
Retirement	45
A change in health of a close family member	44
Pregnancy	40

Source: Holmes, T.H. and Rahe, R.H. (1967)

While these are regarded as highly stressful events in our lives, some can also be occasions of great happiness: pregnancy, marriage, or reuniting after a separation. Have you experienced any of these important life events? Are you about to face one of these major life challenges? Use this space to note your thoughts and feelings about this list.

____

____

____

____

____

Summary

In this chapter, we have identified a transition. A transition can be a stage in your personal development or it can be a major change or challenge in your life. You have looked back over your own life and found your own transition stages and challenges that you overcame. In the next chapter, we will look at the transition process in more detail.

Most people are aware of the problems associated with being overly stressed: It's bad for your health; it prevents you from functioning well; it makes you unhappy. However, a certain level of stress is inevitable and, more importantly, is valuable. It makes you perform well; it gets your adrenaline flowing when you need it.

While there are a number of techniques that will help you cope with stress, understanding transitions will make emergency stress management techniques less necessary. Understanding that major changes in our lives—whether the result of events or of personal development—are natural, and developing skills to cope with them, can minimize stress. Then you will be able to respond better to the challenge of change.

2

The Seven Stages of Transition

One essential part of dealing with any problem is realizing the problem. Since you already know what a transition is, we are now going to break it down further so that you can recognize the stages of a transition. Knowing where you are in a transition, knowing that your feelings will pass, and knowing that your feelings are normal will help you control what is happening and move through the transition easily. We have divided these feelings into seven stages.

The seven stages can be seen in the graph on page 20, which shows how your feelings about yourself might change over the course of a transition. As the graph shows, your self-esteem will rise and fall as you move through the seven stages of transition. To give you an idea of how this might affect you, compare how you feel about yourself on a good day with how you feel on a bad day.

Transition and Your Self-Esteem

Your self-esteem—how you rate yourself or your feelings of self-worth—is very important to how you feel. This can be influenced by such things as your health and lifestyle, your job, and how other people respond to you.

On a Good Day

These are the days when everything goes well. Coworkers, friends, and family are cooperative and show their appreciation of you at work or in your daily life, and you rise to new challenges and enjoy them. You feel good about yourself, as though you could take on anything. And because you feel so strong and positive, it is as if you create your own luck:

everything goes well for you. Again, your situation and the people around you contribute to your sense of self-worth.

Think of a time when you have experienced these feelings of self-worth. Try to pinpoint one or more reasons for your good feelings about yourself.

____

____

____

On a Bad Day

These are the days when nothing goes right. Your family is at odds with you, and you feel tired and unable to cope. Perhaps you are being asked to do more than is reasonable at work or in your daily life. Because you are trying to do too much, you become increasingly tired and suffer feelings of helplessness. The more powerless you feel to change the situation, the more your own self-esteem suffers. If it goes on too long, you can end up feeling worthless—as if it is all your own fault when really it is the situation that has affected your view of yourself.

Can you think of an occasion when you felt like this? Can you pinpoint one or more things that contributed to your feelings about yourself at the time?

____

____

____

These feelings of high and low self-esteem (which everyone experiences) are shown on the left side of the graph on page 20. Look at the graph itself. The line that shows self-esteem starts midpoint and then rises and falls as it passes through the seven stages of transition.

Changes in Self-Esteem During Transitions

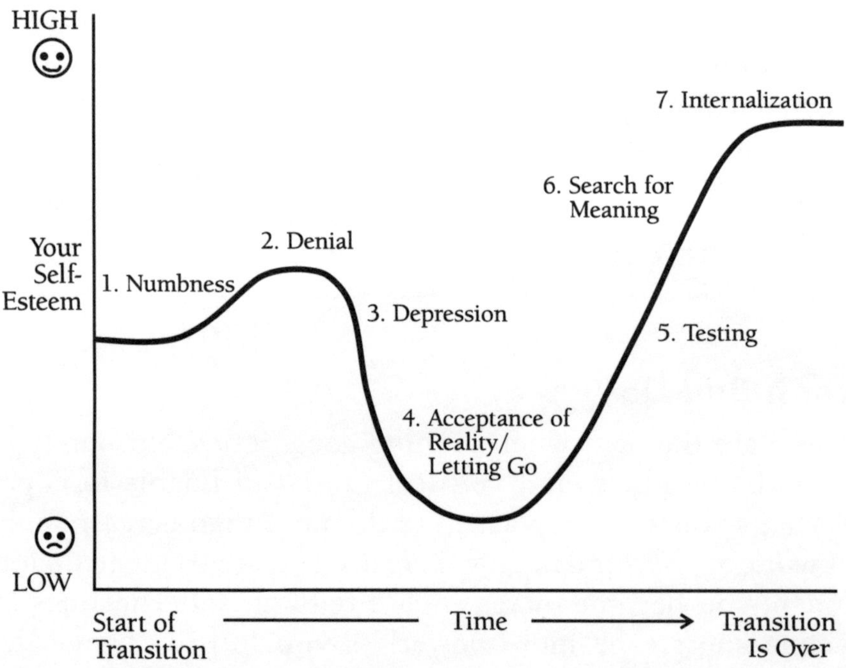

The Seven Stages: What Are They? What Do They Mean?

What you'll read next is our explanation of each of the seven stages. After reading each explanation, try to recall occasions when you have felt like the stage described.

1. Numbness

The first phase is characterized largely by shock. It is a kind of immobilization or a sense of being overwhelmed, of being unable to make plans, unable to reason, and unable to understand. In other words, you freeze up. The more unfamiliar the transition, the stronger the sense of immobilization. In bereavement, for example, many people feel strange because of the absence of feeling, but it is normal to feel numb at this stage. If you feel positive about the transition, however, as you might feel about getting married, this stage will be less intense.

"Oh, no! I can't believe it!" Have you felt like this? When?

____

____

2. *Minimization/Denial*

The movement from numbness to the second stage, denial, does not feel greatly different at the time it is happening. This is because it is characterized by minimization of the change or disruption—even trivialization. Very often you will attempt to deny that the change even exists! Sometimes people project feelings of euphoria, which is great if you've got a new job or a new baby, but may be less appropriate if you've just been fired!

During this stage you may think, "This is not as bad as I expected." However, the apparent ease of the transition is due to the body building up its defenses for the full impact of the transition, which is yet to come. This is often a high-energy stage because with a transition such as bereavement, the person is often at the center of attention with friends and relatives. With a transition such as a promotion, the denial stage may be a refusal to recognize some of the real changes that will take place, such as the loss of comradery with fellow employees, new responsibilities, and the uncertainty about being able to do the new job.

"This is not as bad as I expected." Have you felt like this? When?

____

____

3. *Self-Doubt or Depression*

For most people, the realities of the change and of the resulting stress eventually begin to become apparent. As you become aware that you must make some changes in the way you are living and aware of the realities involved, you sometimes become uncertain. Self-doubt is usually a consequence of feelings of powerlessness—of aspects of your life being out of control. This can happen even when the transition is eagerly anticipated, not only when it is feared. So a longed-for promotion can lead to grave self-doubts about being capable of doing the job.

This stage has occasional high-energy periods, often characterized by anger, before you slide back into a feeling of hopelessness. You may become frustrated because it seems difficult to know how to best cope with the new life requirements, the new ways of being, and the new relationships that have been established.

"I'm not sure if I'm up to it." Have you felt like this? When?

____

____

4. *Acceptance of Reality/Letting Go*

As you gradually become aware of the new reality, you can move into the fourth phase, which is accepting the transition for what it is. Letting go may be a gradual "three steps forward—two steps back" type of process. Someone who has been divorced may feel successful in letting go until he or she sees the ex-spouse with a new partner. This may be quite painful and can make him or her think, "This is awful. I thought I was through this, but I'm not."

Through the first three phases, there was a kind of attachment, whether conscious or not, to the past situation.

To move from phase three to phase four involves a process of unhooking from the past and saying, "Well, here I am. Here is what I have. I know I can survive. I may not be sure of what I want yet, but I will be okay. There is life out there waiting for me." As this is accepted as the new reality, your feelings begin to rise once more, and optimism becomes possible.

"Let it happen; this is it." Have you felt like this? When?

---

5. *Testing*

You become much more active and start testing yourself in the new situation, trying out new behaviors, new lifestyles, and new ways of coping with the transition. After a divorce, this is often the stage when people begin dating again. There is also a tendency at this point to stereotype, to seek categories and classifications for the ways other people react to the new situation. There is much personal energy available during this phase, and it sometimes shows itself in irritation or tears.

"Perhaps if I try . . . " Have you felt like this? When?

---

6. *Search for Meaning*

Following the burst of activity and self-testing, there is a gradual shift toward understanding, when you may ask, "Is this right for me?" or "What does this mean for me?" You need to know the meaning of these changes—how they will affect your future and your whole sense of who you are. If it is not "right for me," there will be further testing of alternatives until one is found that is right and that fits with your sense of self. It is only when you have a sense of what these changes mean and what their meaning for your life is that you can move on to the next stage.

"Is this right?" Have you felt like this? When?

____

____

7. Internalization

Finally, if the transition has been one you have ultimately accepted, you move into the final phase of internalizing the meanings and incorporating them into your changed behavior, routines, or lifestyle. The person who, after losing his or her job, continues to leave home at the same time each morning and return the same time each evening is having difficulty with this final stage. In fact, he or she is having difficulty with the whole transition.

This person may be stuck at the denial stage or fluctuating between denial and self-doubt because he or she cannot yet accept the new reality. Acceptance is crucial before moving forward to the final stages of transition and the restoration of self-esteem. Once you have fully accepted (internalized) the stages of change you have been through, you can begin to look forward in a more positive frame of mind and start to build on the new strengths you have developed.

"Now I can see the way ahead." Have you felt like this? When?

____

____

Rarely—if ever—does a person move neatly from phase to phase. For example, one person may never get beyond minimization or denial. Another may just stop at depression. Yet another may experience a major setback just as things begin to look up and revert to a less active phase. But we believe that for a transition to be effectively managed, all seven phases must be worked through. Often we try to avoid the depression stage—or help others avoid it—to prevent our own embarrassment or to cover up our feelings of inadequacy. If you allow yourself to grieve, you can move toward the new opportunities opened up to us by the transition.

When you do allow yourself to move forward and finally reach the stage of internalization, it can be like a rebirth or an emergence from a long, dark hibernation into the bright light. You can feel like the brand-new butterfly that has metamorphosed over the months from a pupa into a splendid, bright creature in a new world of freedom.

Understanding the stages of transition will help you cope with your feelings and move forward. Think of a transition that you have experienced—a move to a new school or neighborhood, a change in a relationship, a change of occupation, or some other personal change. Review the seven stages on the graph on the next page and make some notes on it to see if your transition fits.

Give your transition a name. Does it fit in with the pattern?

____

____

Each time you are invited to think about a transition, you will be given a space to write down the name you give it. (There is a more detailed plan for dealing with a major transition later in the book.) Reflecting on your past experiences will help you prepare for this.

Changes in Self-Esteem During Transitions

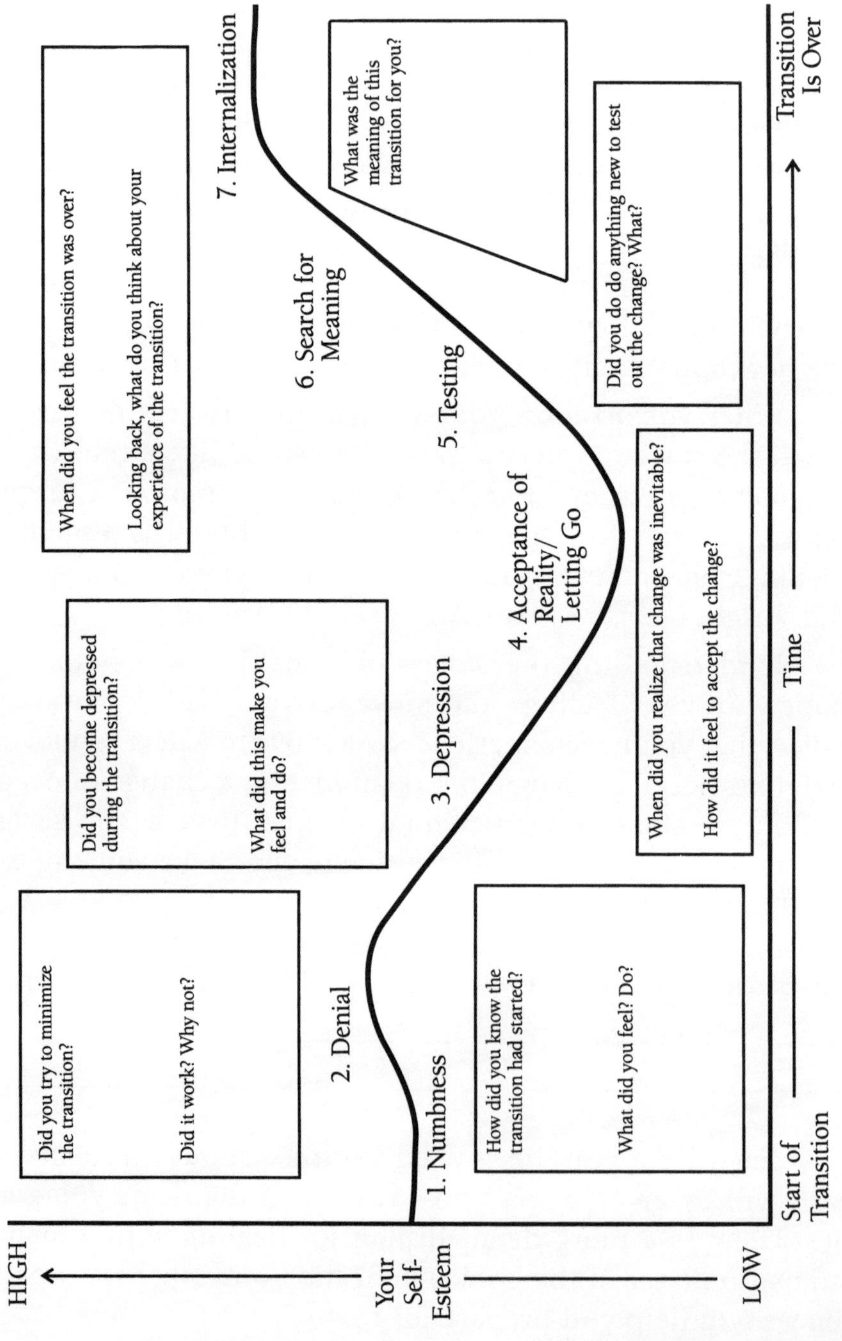

Summary

You are now aware of the seven stages of transition:

- Numbness
- Minimization/Denial
- Self-doubt or Depression
- Acceptance of Reality/Letting Go
- Testing
- Search for Meaning
- Internalization

You know that these are common features of transitions, and your knowledge may help you move more smoothly through the process next time. Like all skills, it takes practice. We are not suggesting, for example, that you can bypass the stage of depression simply by knowing it exists, but at least you needn't feel guilty—you can work on overcoming the depression rather than covering it up.

3

Some of Your Finest Transitional Moments

This chapter is entirely practical. It may take you several hours or several days. If possible, find a block of uninterrupted free time before you tackle this chapter. You now have an opportunity to relive, in detail, some transitions you have experienced. This will build on your understanding of the seven stages of a transition and will allow you to understand how you respond to change.

You have already thought about some of the transitions you have experienced; now dig deeper into your memory to make a fuller list. Rather than trying to dredge items from an unwilling memory, use some of the following ideas to take your mind back. Try to find time to indulge yourself in this activity. The ultimate benefit to you may be very great.

My Life Plan—Past, Present, and Future

Pictures of the Past

Get out your old photo albums and browse through them. Think about the kinds of transitions that were taking place. Look at old films or videos.

Written Records

If you keep old letters, read through a few. What did people say to you? How have things changed? Look through your old diaries.

Musical Memories

Listen to the music you used to enjoy at different stages of your life.

The Places You Went

Go somewhere you used to go. If you haven't been there for a while, there will be plenty of opportunity to say "It's all changed" and to think about how you have changed.

The People You Knew

Reminisce about the good old days and bad old days—if possible, with others who were there.

Personal Project: Creating a Life Plan

Using these memories and others, fill in the Life Plan on page 33. Record all of the memories you can possibly conjure. Remember to include the appropriate Stages of Personal Development (see page 8) as well as Major Life Events (see page 14). This is a long activity, so allow sufficient time to complete it.

The example on page 32 should give you some ideas for your own Life Plan. Margaret's Life Plan raises a series of questions for her. What happened to her childhood friends? Will her children leaving home mean she has more leisure time? Should she use some of this time to trace those old friends or make new ones? Will her job be as fulfilling and demanding as raising a family, or will she have time for new hobbies and activities? What should she do to plan for the changes ahead?

Now do your own Life Plan on page 33. Mark all your transitions on the age scale, and make notes in the spaces provided.

Sample Completed Life Plan
(Margaret's as she approaches 50)

<table>
<tr><td>Age</td><td>0-10</td><td>11-20</td><td>21-30</td><td>31-40</td><td>41-50</td><td>51-70</td></tr>
<tr><td>Transitions</td><td>1, 2, 3</td><td>4, 5, 6</td><td>7, 8, 9</td><td>10, 11, 12</td><td>13, 14, 15</td><td></td></tr>
<tr><td colspan="7">1. My birth!</td></tr>
<tr><td colspan="7">2. Started school. I loved my first teacher, Mrs. Jones.</td></tr>
<tr><td colspan="7">3. My sister's birth. That put my nose out of joint for a while! Seems I was jealous and used to hide her so Mom couldn't find her!</td></tr>
<tr><td colspan="7">4. Went to the big school. Hated it at first; it was so huge. Eventually made good friends. Wonder what happened to them?</td></tr>
<tr><td colspan="7">5. Left school.</td></tr>
<tr><td colspan="7">6. Started work in a local accountant's office.</td></tr>
<tr><td colspan="7">7. Got married–parents not happy at first.</td></tr>
<tr><td colspan="7">8. Birth of first child, Lisa. Quit work.</td></tr>
<tr><td colspan="7">9. Birth of second child, James.</td></tr>
<tr><td colspan="7">10. Moved to new house.</td></tr>
<tr><td colspan="7">11. Returned to work.</td></tr>
<tr><td colspan="7">12. Both parents required assistance. Had a terrible time coping with full-time work, running a home, and looking after them every day. Lived with father and nursed him for his last two weeks. Both parents died within six months.</td></tr>
<tr><td colspan="7">13. Found a better job.</td></tr>
<tr><td colspan="7">14. Children starting to leave home: Lisa is married and is working; James is a student.</td></tr>
<tr><td colspan="7">15. Where am I now? What next? I suppose I have to get used to an empty house and decide whether to develop this new job into a career–that's one transition. Then there will be retirement, possibly weddings and grandchildren–that's a whole series of changes coming up.</td></tr>
</table>

Personal Life Plan

Age	0-10	11-20	21-30	31-40	41-50	51-60
Transitions						

AGE	NOTES
0-5	
6-10	
11-15	
16-20	
21-25	
26-30	
31-35	
36-40	
41-45	
46-50	
51-55	
56-60	

Note: There will still be transitions after 60, so continue on another sheet of paper if you wish.

How many transitions have you marked on your Life Plan?

___

How many are stages in personal development (which everyone experiences), and how many are major life events?

___

Which transitions do you feel good about?

___

Which transitions were difficult for you?

___

Did anything surprise you?

___

What was your most interesting discovery?

___

How do you react to looking at your own Life Plan and your transitions?

___

___

___

Now choose two of the transitions that were important to you. Try to choose two with different characteristics; for example, choose one you felt good about and one that involved change that was difficult or that you were reluctant to accept. We will use the experiences you gained from these two transitions to find out how you can build on your strengths to cope with future transitions. Give a name to each transition that you have chosen.

My two transitions are

1. ____________________

2. ____________________

Look at each one in detail by noting some answers to the following questions. Use your photos and your recent reminiscences to help you remember. Also apply the Seven Stages of Transition to remind you how you might have felt.

Transition 1 ____________________

What do I remember?

____

____

____

How was I different afterward from before?

____

____

Did it cause me any difficulty?

____

____

Did anything or anybody help? If so, how?

____

____

When did I feel comfortable again and accept the new situation?

____

How do I feel about that transition now?

____

____

Transition 2 ______________________

What do I remember?

____

____

____

How was I different afterward from before?

____

____

Did it cause me any difficulty?

____

____

Did anything or anybody help? If so, how?

____

____

When did I feel comfortable again and accept the new situation?

____

How do I feel about that transition now?

____

____

By considering these two transitions, you have started to build a picture of how you deal with change.

Note any characteristics you recognize in your response to transitions.

____

____

You may have noted that you are generally optimistic about life's changes or that wariness is always apparent in the early stages of transition. Note them in case there are characteristics you would like to build on or change. The next chapter goes into this in greater detail.

Summary

Now you know how you have responded to transitions in the past and perhaps what is happening to you at the present time. You may feel that your past responses have been healthy, or you may feel that they have been unhealthy.

4

Taking the Upset Out of Upheaval

This chapter will help you clarify how you cope with transitions, and will suggest how to develop these and other skills to minimize the upset and upheaval.

The text will address how you can

- Know what you want
- Know your new situation
- Know who can help you
- Look after yourself
- Leave the past behind

Learning to Cope

Here are some questions about how you cope with transitions. Think about your own coping styles and your way of life, and then apply the questions to one of the transitions you thought about in the previous chapter. (Use the transition you think is most characteristic of your style.)

Knowing What I Want

Is this transition something I want to happen?

____

Am I somebody who "makes things happen" rather than one who sits back and lets things happen? Do I know what I want and make efforts to achieve it?

____

____

Do I know what I would like to get out of this new situation?

____

____

Do I know what I do not want from this new situation?

____

____

If I feel under stress, do I know what I can do to help myself?

____

____

If you answered yes to a question, you are obviously coping well with that area of the transition. If you answered no, you may find some of the ideas below helpful. (Even a yes answer may benefit from new ideas.) Try to develop skills so that you can answer yes to more questions—then you will be well on the way to coping competently with transitions.

Knowing Myself Better

Often you do not choose transitions. This sometimes makes it difficult to accept the change, but you basically have only three choices:

- Refuse to accept it
- Accept it but just put up with it
- Accept it and try to benefit from it

The first will bring nothing but bad feelings and is unlikely to reverse the changes; it probably means that you will be unable to cope with the tasks facing you in the new situation. The second will help you survive. The third will help you not only survive but benefit and grow from the experience.

Asking "What is the worst thing that can happen?" sometimes helps you face your fears. Anxieties are usually based on generalized, unidentified, and fantastic fears. Actually facing up to the worst that can happen may help you to identify specific possibilities. If you think and talk about these possibilities, you'll probably find that they are not that terrible or that they are unlikely to materialize. And even if the worst does happen, at least you've prepared yourself.

Making things happen in the way you want them to rather than waiting for things to happen to you is being proactive. It is an approach that believes that you can always make things more like you want them to be; that you can be more in charge of yourself and situations; that you and others can gain from being more self-directed; and that you can be someone who does things for yourself rather than someone who has things done to you. It is not about being aggressive or ruthless, but rather about choosing, acting, and growing positively. The more you are thinking, deciding, and doing for yourself, the more useful you are going to be to yourself, to others, and to society.

How Proactive Am I?

Answer these questions as honestly as you can.

Could I make a decision to change something in my life and follow through on it?

____

Do I spend a lot of time worrying about decisions?

____

Do I rely on other people to make decisions for me?

____

Do I keep my worries to myself?

____

Do I know how to help myself deal with decisions?

Looking at your answers will tell you if you are satisfied with your ability to handle decisions. All change involves making decisions: Sometimes they are easy, sometimes painful. Letting other people make decisions for you does not help you manage your own transition and grow in the ways you want. However, there are a number of things you can do that can help you be more proactive and feel more in control.

Try the following useful guidelines for a start.

- Look after yourself.
- Manage your transitions one at a time.
- Don't blame or punish yourself.
- Manage decisions one at a time—or decide to not make a decision!
- Avoid overly complicating the issue by trying to deal with too many things at once, and avoid situations in which you feel stressed and may overreact.
- Always remember that time will help as you progress through a transition, although the more you can do to actively help yourself, the better.

It is worth looking at each of these in more detail. The following activities will help you identify ways in which you can help yourself if you are facing a transition or if you are in the middle of one now.

Looking After Yourself

To begin with, answer the following questions.

Do I exercise regularly or have a fitness program?

Do I eat regularly and sensibly?

Do I have a regular routine?

Do I have places to go to, people to be with, or comfortable situations that give me a secure base?

Do I give myself rewards if I'm going through a bad time?

Do I have people who will take care of me when I need them?

Am I able to "survive" during hard economic times until better times come?

Do I know the times and situations when I am likely to be at my lowest?

When I feel low, do I do any of the following?

- Skip meals
- Cut exercise
- Abandon my daily routine
- Sleep badly or not long enough
- Avoid friends
- Neglect myself

If you answered yes to any of the items on the last list, think carefully about the advice that follows. Looking after yourself is the first and most important practical step to take to help you deal with change.

Personal Project

Complete the simple timetable of a week's activities on the next page. Mark your most basic routines—times of going to bed and getting up, meal times, and other regular activities, such as going to work.

Now list any regular exercise times. If you normally walk the dog each morning, mark the time this occupies. If you attend an exercise class or do your exercises at home each lunchtime, fill it in. Be truthful! Exercise is often one of the first casualties during times of stress! The timetable should show a typical week's activity; it will not be useful if you are dishonest with yourself.

Using a different color, mark in the times when you normally relax. Include anything that you feel helps you relax, from gardening to reading or watching a favorite TV program.

Now think of a week from the past when things were going well—a time when you felt on top of things, when every day was a good day. Would that week's timetable be different? Were you exercising more? Spending more time relaxing? Eating meals regularly?

Your ability to cope with stress depends on your physical well-being. Because you need to be fit and healthy to cope effectively with transitions, regular exercise and a healthful diet are essential coping skills. It is particularly important to eat well during a transition, when you may have neither the time nor the inclination to do so.

Using your Weekly Activity Timetable, and your knowledge of yourself, write down the bad habits you fall into during times of stress. For instance, do you start drinking more alcohol in the hope that it will relax you? Do you find

Weekly Activity Timetable

Mon																		
Tues																		
Wed																		
Thur																		
Fri																		
Sat																		
Sun																		

☐ Sleeping ☐ Meals ☐ Exercise ☐ Traveling ☐ Relaxation ☐ Other: ____________

This timetable shows an eighteen-hour day. Mark your own hours at the top, so that, if you are a shift worker, for example, your day might run from 4 a.m. to 10 p.m. Using different colors for each activity (listed above) will help you see what you do when.

yourself snacking between meals when you are not really hungry?

What can you do to avoid these bad habits? What can you do to eat and drink more sensibly?

You could get a book on exercise or healthful eating to motivate yourself. You could join a gym or exercise class. If you feel particularly unfit, see your doctor for advice on how to get fit.

What other things could you do to stay healthy and well?

Relaxation techniques are also well worth learning, as they can help prevent you from becoming too uptight about things that are bothering you. Make a point to spend a little time relaxing each day. It sometimes helps to give yourself a treat—an enjoyable outing, a visit with a friend, or the purchase of something small that you will enjoy.

What other things could I do to relax?

Exercise is a good way to relax and take your mind off things. Racquetball, walking, swimming, yoga—almost any form of exercise will promote both physical and mental relaxation. Other forms of relaxation include gardening, reading, watching a movie—anything that will take your mind off your problems.

Routine and structure in one's life can be of great assistance at times of transition. If our internal world is in disarray, keeping our external world in order can help. Look for the "anchor points" in your life—the zones of stability that you can be sure of while all else is changing. These range from the most basic of routines such as going to bed at a regular hour to mundane rituals such as making meals, shopping, and performing household chores. For example, the daily routine of delivering the children to school and the ritual exchange of greetings and news with other parents are trivial events but ones that can be a lifeline during difficult periods.

Recognize these daily routines and look on them as helpful anchor points in your day rather than as nuisances. Make a start with a new timetable now (one is provided on the next page), and mark your routines on it. This time, think about how to make these routines work for you: If your bedtime changes every day, think of the most sensible time to get to bed to ensure that you get enough rest and decide to make it a ritual.

Give your new timetable the heading "How I Can Help Myself" Now look at your answers to the questions about exercise, eating, and relaxation. Make space on your timetable for your new ideas on eating well, exercising regularly, and relaxing.

How I Can Help Myself Timetable

Mon																			
Tues																			
Wed																			
Thur																			
Fri																			
Sat																			
Sun																			

☐ Sleeping ☐ Meals ☐ Exercise ☐ Traveling ☐ Relaxation ☐ Other: ____________

Knowing Others Who Can Help

Here is another set of questions to answer.

Who can I depend on in a crisis?

____

Who can I discuss my concerns with?

____

Who can recognize my strengths and make me feel valued?

____

Who can give me any information I need?

____

Who will challenge me and make me face things?

____

Who can I share good times and experiences with?

____

There is now considerable evidence to show that talking problems through with people (friends, peers, parents, colleagues, or even strangers) helps reduce stress at times of change. Having a support group is a valuable asset. Your own support group could include your husband or wife, colleagues, a mentor, parents, relatives, or friends. Consider sources of help available to you and to realize the importance of developing a range of "helpers" rather than being dependent on just one or two people for everything.

Obviously, most of our support comes from friends or those sympathetic to us, but it is also important to be challenged. Someone who can make us face things can actually provoke us into examining our ideas and actions in a very positive way.

The kinds of support I need:

____

____

____

____

People who can provide me with this support:

____

____

____

____

Is there a space in your timetable where you could plan to make contact with friends by visiting them, telephoning them, or inviting them out? Why not mark it in? All too often, at times of stress, you cut yourself off from friends who could be most helpful. An evening out with a friend is relaxing and helps restore your sense of self-esteem at a time when you might need it.

Plan: Don't Be Rushed

Manage Your Transitions One at a Time

This might be easier said than done, as some major life events may involve several kinds of transitions. For example, a move to a new home can mean searching for suitable accommodations, as well as adapting to new patterns of travel, finding new centers for shopping and leisure, adapting to a new job, and making new friends and contacts.

It will help you to identify each transition and deal with it separately, one at a time. It will not help you if you feel pressured into hasty decisions simply because of the sheer amount of change going on. If possible, take these major changes one at a time. This might mean planning ahead so that you have time to settle into a new home and surroundings before you start the search for a job or a new school for the children.

Have you experienced times when many transitions were going on? How well did you cope?

Don't Blame or Punish Yourself

When things go wrong—as they are bound to sometimes—don't waste time in destructive self-criticism. This just undermines your self-esteem even further. Rather, take time out to think about the new situation and how to best deal with it; give yourself a little treat to boost your self-esteem, and you will be surprised how much easier it is to deal with whatever you feel has gone wrong.

Are you prone to self-blame? What can you do next time to avoid it?

Manage Your Decisions One at a Time

It is surprising how many decisions can be safely postponed until you feel better able to make them. This is not the same as letting events or other people make your decisions for you, dodging the whole issue, and putting it off indefinitely. Rather, it is the clever knack of recognizing which decisions have the highest priority and must be dealt with now and which decisions can safely wait until you have more information or until a decision has become absolutely necessary.

Don't let other people push you into making a decision you do not feel ready to make. If necessary, tell yourself and other people that you are busy dealing with another decision that must come first and that you will deal with the next one when you are ready.

Do you experience the feeling of being overwhelmed by too many decisions at once? What can you do to deal with this problem in the future?

You could make a list of all the decisions you need to make on one piece of paper and then write it out again in order of priority.

Avoid Overcomplication and Overreaction

The same advice applies in this case, with the added ingredient of stress. If you feel harassed by a particular situation and pushed into making a decision you don't feel you can make, avoid it or defuse it by simply saying, "I am not going to make a decision on this right now. I will let you know when I have made my decision." This straightforward approach helps other people recognize your right to make your own decisions when you are ready.

Can you recognize when you are feeling stressed and sidestep or defuse the situation?

Remember That Time Will Help

Time will help you come to terms with any new situation. But in order to come through a transition feeling that you have learned from the experience, you need to help yourself along the way. (Remember the person who got stuck at the stage of denial?) All of the reading and thinking that you are doing now will help you to manage change in a proactive way—for yourself.

What has been the most important thing you have learned or fully understood for your own experience of transitions so far?

____

____

____

____

Summary

In this chapter we have looked in some detail at useful techniques for coping with difficult decision-making during times of transition. Perhaps you already use some of these techniques but can now recognize when you are using them and why. If these techniques are new to you, don't wait for a major life event to try them out! Start putting them into practice right away; practicing on the simple decisions is good preparation for the hard ones! In either case, you should be more aware of how you generally cope with decisions and change—and better equipped to be proactive about both in the future.

5

The Challenge of Change

All of the things you have learned so far, such as looking after yourself and creating a support network, will help you deal with future change.

How else can you prepare yourself for the transitions that lie ahead? One of the keys is to recognize when you are coming up to a transition so you can prepare yourself. The second is to know in advance what you want out of the new situation.

Knowing My New Situation

What will I call the new situation?

____

Do I know how I will be expected to behave in the new situation?

____

____

Is there any way I can try out the new situation in advance?

____

____

What do I hope for out of the new situation?

____

____

What things can I do to be more aware of what I want from the new situation?

____

____

Talk to friends or other people who are aware of your situation and about what you might expect to gain or lose. Discuss ways in which you can manage the change so it goes the way you want.

Think forward to what the new situation will be like. Collect as much information as you can about the new situation. What will be expected of you? What is regarded as normal in this situation? What do others expect? This will give you a chance to ask the following questions:

Will I need to change in any way?

____

____

Do I want to change in any way?

____

____

Am I prepared to change in any way?

____

If the answer to the last question is no, you should examine your motives for refusing to change. Because all transition involves change of some kind, it is important to accept change and make it work in the way you want. Some people find it difficult to accept change because of their attachment to their old situation. Is this you?

Leaving the Past Behind

Do I hang on to the past or easily leave one situation and move to another?

____

Do I often think, "It's not fair. This should not happen to me!"?

____

Do I want to get through the bad patches, leave the past behind, and carry on with what lies ahead?

____

Am I able to find opportunities to express anger or other strong feelings in ways that help?

____

Sometimes you think, feel, talk, and act in a way that "locks" you into a situation that you liked or in which you were secure and comfortable. You don't want to move; you just hang on. Yet hanging on to one situation, whether physically, psychologically, or emotionally, can prevent growth and development.

There are a number of ways you might respond to leaving the past behind. You can

- Wish it hadn't passed—but it has!
- Remember the good things—but they are gone, and if you spend too much time remembering, you are missing new opportunities now and in the future.
- Refuse to think or talk about it—this probably means that you are a slave of the past and not the master. Talking about the good and the bad can free you to move on.

- Not express your feelings of sadness, anger, or whatever else you may feel—unexpressed feelings are again likely to control you or block future opportunities.
- Recognize that something good has gone—appreciate it, talk about it, but leave that stage behind for the next.

What can I do to ensure that I leave the past behind in a positive way?

____

____

____

____

Of course there is another reason for reluctance to change—fear of the future. And because you cannot know for sure how things will work out, this uncertainty is one of the major features of any transition. But you can prepare yourself to both deal with the uncertainty and reduce it. As you have seen throughout this workbook, many aspects of transition have both a positive and a negative side; they can be alarming but also exciting.

The Chinese have two words for crisis: One means "danger," the other "opportunity." All transitions, however unwelcome, offer the prospect of growth and development. For example, while few would choose to become unemployed, unemployment does offer the opportunity for a personal reevaluation. Many exciting new businesses have been started by people who saw this as the only way of breaking out of unemployment.

Transitions are challenging, but it is only by responding to challenges that you realize your full potential—that you really achieve what you are capable of.

Personal Project: Seeing the Transition Positively

Think again about the transition you used at the beginning of the last chapter. Then write down as many points as you can come up with in the two columns. However, before you enter an item in the "Don't Like" column, you must put one in the "Do Like" column.

Evaluation of a Transition

Things I Like (or Might Come to Like)	Things I Don't Like
____________________	____________________
____________________	____________________
____________________	____________________
____________________	____________________
____________________	____________________
____________________	____________________
____________________	____________________
____________________	____________________

Hopefully, you have come up with some positive aspects of the transition. Usually when you stop being negative and force yourself to be positive, you can see the good in situations.

Now answer the following questions; they should encourage you to come up with even more positive ideas. If you find it difficult to think of positive aspects of your transition, discuss it with someone else; perhaps he or she can see it from a different angle.

What is one thing I hope to gain (or have gained) by moving into my new situation?

____

What opportunities do I now have that I didn't have or hadn't thought of before?

____

____

____

Is there something new I have learned about myself?

____

____

____

In what ways am I different now from how I was before?

____

____

____

____

Even if you find it difficult to see any new opportunities ahead, remember all the ways in which you can influence change by acting proactively for yourself. When you are facing the prospect of a transition in your life and when you are experiencing maximum uncertainty is the time to start reducing the uncertainty by planning to do the things that will help you. Remember your How I Can Help Myself Timetable, the anchor points and the helpful routines, the importance of rest, exercise, and good food? Commit to a timetable when you will start to make these changes.

Self-Improvement Action Plan

This week I will ____

____

____

Starting day ____

This month I will _______________________________________

____

____

Starting day ____

Next month I will _______________________________________

____

____

Starting day ____

In a year, I will be better at ____________________________

____

____

Summary

Think of the Chinese symbols for crisis: One means disaster, the other means opportunity. Keep them in mind when you face times of transition, and concentrate on making the most of the opportunities presented to you.

If change is inevitable, then it is important that you know how to deal with leaving the past behind and facing the uncertainty of the future. You can develop ways to help yourself manage the transition smoothly and positively.

With your new plans to look forward to, you will consider the challenge of change in the next chapter. Remember, transitions aren't all bad—far from it.

6

Your Next Transition

We have told you all we think you need to know about making transitions. Hopefully, while working through the book, you have discovered that you knew most of it already. Now you should be able to apply it.

Expectations

To enable you to do that, this chapter invites you to think ahead. Anticipate change that you may face in the near future. Perhaps you are thinking about getting married, working overseas, or are contemplating some other change. Take this opportunity to plan how to ease yourself through the difficult stages and to ultimately benefit from the challenge.

Personal Project

We now invite you to take your time to reflect on what you have learned from this workbook and complete the following quiz, which asks you to comment on your feelings about and your expectations of this expected transition.

Transition Assessment Quiz

Feelings and Expectations Before the Event

Am I anxious about anything?

____

Am I excited about anything?

____

What am I looking forward to?

____

What will I miss?

____

What do I know about the new situation? What have I done to try to find out about it?

____

Will there be any difficulties? If so, what?

____

Is there anything I can do now to prepare? If so, what?

____

What help will be available if I need it? (Use this space to write a list of your anchor points, the people in your support group, treats you could give yourself, etc.)

____

____

____

____

____

____

____

____

____

____

Transition Chart

Use the boxes in the chart on the next page to show the events that you think will occur at each of the seven stages of the transition. (This way, you will be prepared for the low point in your self-esteem, and it will not take you by surprise.)

Changes in Self-Esteem During Transitions

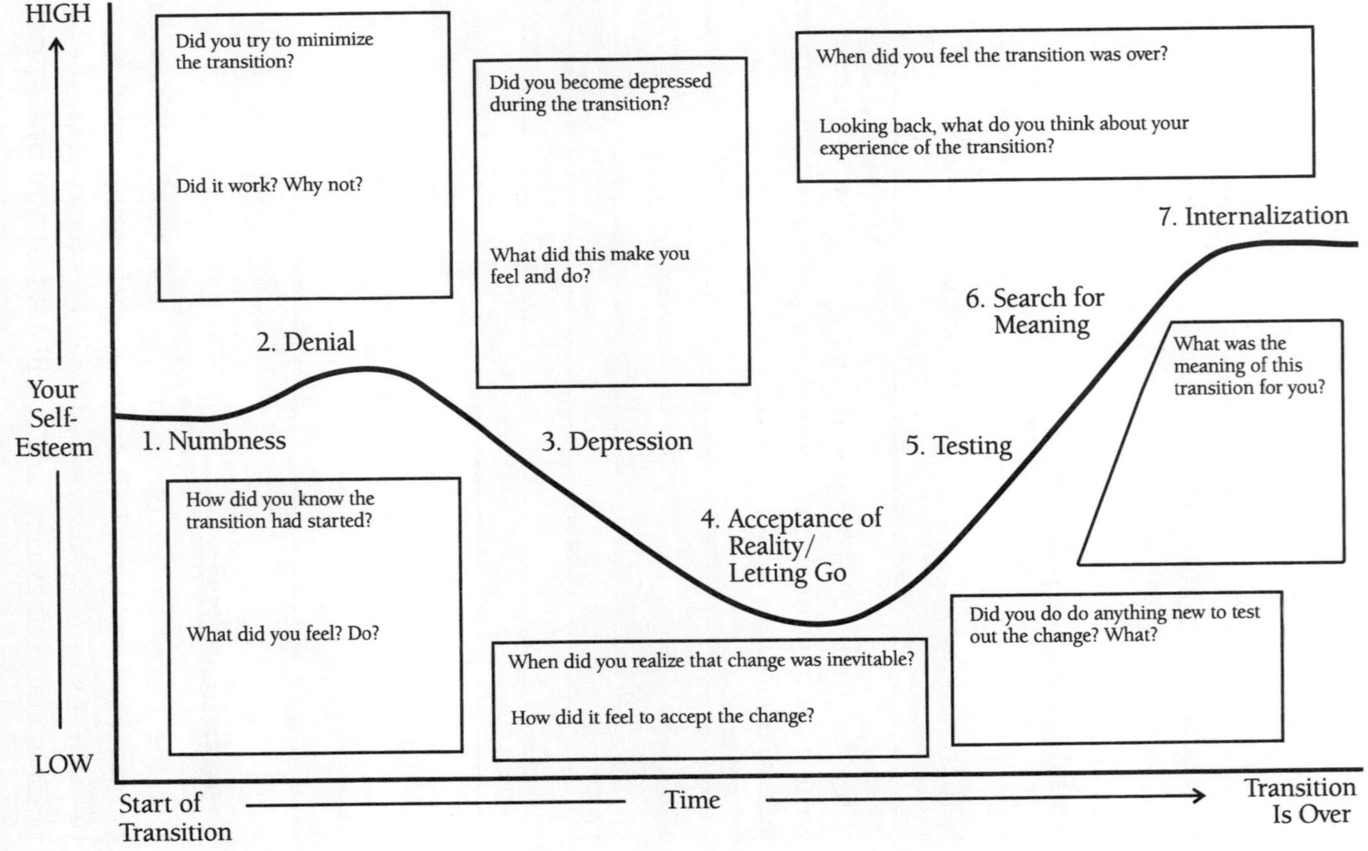

Just thinking about your next transition will help you deal with it. When your next transition does actually occur, write down your feelings on the following Transition Record.

Try to keep this book's copies of the chart and record as your masters and make photocopies to use with each new transition.

Transition Record

Fill in the seven stages chart and the table as you progress through the transition. Analyzing what happens as it happens will not only help you with your next transition, but with all of your future transitions.

Transition Table

Ongoing Record During Transition

Feelings:	
1. At the start	
2. After one day	
3. After two days	
4. After one week	
5. Later (say when)	
6. Later (say when)	
How did you behave at each of the above stages? Were you restless, relaxed, anxious, etc.?	1. 2. 3. 4. 5. 6.
Difficulties encountered:	
By you	
By others	
How you coped	
How you saw others cope	

Coping Techniques

Try each of these, if appropriate, and note whether it helps or not.	
1. Discuss how you feel with somebody. Does it help?	
2. Find somewhere quiet to relax. Does it help?	
3. Try thinking about the way things were prior to the transition. Does it help?	
4. Try some physical activity, e.g., exercise, gardening, decorating. Does it help?	
5. Try thinking of all the best things about the new situation. Does it help?	
6. Try giving yourself a treat—something you really enjoy. Does it help?	
7. Anything else you found helpful?	

Moving Through the Transition

When did you begin to feel relaxed at home or adjusted to the new situation?	
How long had the transition lasted?	
What had helped you to feel at home?	
Had you done anything to help yourself?	

Moving Through the Transition (continued)

Had others done anything to help you?	
Are there any differences between a. What you expected?	
b. What actually happened?	

What the Transition Taught Me

What did I learn about myself?

____

____

About other people?

____

____

About moving into new situations in the future?

____

____

Congratulations! You've passed another milestone in your life. We hope you have gained from it.

Summary

Planning carefully for your next transition will help you move through it more easily. You will be more likely to expect the unexpected, you will be ready for the low points in your self-esteem, and you will concentrate on the opportunities the transition presents.

7

Helping Others

Everyone goes through transitions, and by now, you have some expertise in the area. If you know people who are having difficulty with transitions, you may be able to help them. Here are some of the things you can do.

- Listen to them talk about the transition, and try to bring out their feelings about it.
- Sensitively suggest some of the strategies for coping with transitions that you think will be useful.
- Give them a treat—this is even better than getting them to give one to themselves.
- Offer practical help.

Add any other ideas below:

____

____

Do you know any people who are going through a transition? If so, who?

____

How can you help them?

____

____

____

When will you help them?

____

Not only will helping other people make you feel good, but there is also a chance they'll help you out in the future.

A Final Comment: Metamorphosis

A pupa metamorphosing into a butterfly is a natural process—it is something that must happen for the insect to become beautiful, to be able to fly, to realize its potential.

This is a good symbol for you when facing transitions because, to realize life's potential, you need to change, and change is inevitable. Even so, it often causes stress and worry.

Having worked through this book, we hope you will have developed the following knowledge and skills:

- You are able to recognize a transition and to know whether it arises from a major life event or a stage of personal development.
- You know that there are seven stages through which you must pass in a transition: numbness, minimization/denial, self-doubt or depression, acceptance of reality/letting go, testing, search for meaning, and internalization.
- You can apply the above to transitions in your own life.
- You are aware of the stress you may face during a transition, and you now have ways of coping with it.
- You know that transitions present opportunities for you to make the most of.
- You have skills that enable you to handle transitions well.

Use this knowledge and these skills whenever you face a difficult transition and, as you already know, things will become easier.

[illegible]

[illegible]

[illegible]

- [illegible]
- [illegible]
- [illegible]

[illegible]

- [illegible]
- [illegible]

[illegible]

Bibliography

Gould, R.L. *Transformations: Growth & Change in Adult Life.* New York: Simon & Schuster, 1978.

Holmes, T.H., and Rahe, R.H. "Social Readjustment Rating Scale." *Journal of Psychomatic Research, II* (1967), pp. 213-218.

Hopson, Barrie, and Mike Scally. *Build Your Own Rainbow.* San Diego, CA: Pfeiffer & Company, 1993.

McGee-Cooper, Ann, Duane Trammell, and Barbara Lau. *You Don't Have to Go Home From Work Exhausted!* Dallas, Texas: Bowen & Rogers, 1990.

Schein, Edgar. *Career Anchors.* San Diego, CA: Pfeiffer & Company, 1993.

About the Authors

Dr. Barrie Hopson

Barrie is joint chairman of Lifeskills Learning Ltd. Previously he founded the Counseling and Career Development Unit at Leeds University and was the first director until 1984. He has worked widely as a consultant to industrial and educational organizations in the United Kingdom, the United States of America, and Europe. He was responsible for setting up the first career counseling service in British industry in 1970 (at Imperial Chemical Industry) and has since helped a number of organizations in different countries to set up career counseling and career management systems. He is a professional associate of the National Training Laboratories for Applied Behavioral Science in Washington, D.C., a fellow of the British Psychological Society, and of the British Institute of Management.

He has written twenty-two books and numerous articles on personal and career development, marriage, lifeskills teaching, quality service, transition, and change management and generic training skills.

Mike Scally

Mike is joint chairman of Lifeskills Learning Ltd. He combines management training with writing and lecturing. He was Deputy Director of the Counseling and Career Development Unit at Leeds University in 1976 and was involved with its training programs and national projects until 1984.

He has extensive training experience with many of the United Kingdom's major companies and an international reputation in the field of education. He serves on the management committees of and is consultant to many national groups—promoting development education and training at home and abroad.

Mike Scally has written twelve books and many articles on career management, customer service, and lifeskills teaching.